Explorers & Exploration

The Travels of
Marco Polo

By Alex Bandon
Illustrated by Patrick O'Brien

Steadwell
Books

Raintree Steck-Vaughn Publishers
A Harcourt Company

Austin · New York
www.steck-vaughn.com

Illustration Acknowledgments:
pp 5, 23, 32, and 36, New York Public Library Picture Collection; pp 15, 16, 20, and 29, John Blazejewski; pp 24–25, Art Resources.
All other artwork is by Patrick O'Brien.

Contents

A Legend Is Born

In 1296, more than 700 years ago, a rich man sat in a prison in what is now Italy. He was 42 years old. War was raging between the city of Genoa and his home city of Venice. The rich man had been captured when his ships lost a big sea battle.

While in prison, the rich man made friends with a man named Rustichello. He was a famous writer from Pisa, a city in Italy. Rustichello had been in prison for ten years. The rich man started telling Rustichello about the wonderful things he had seen all over the world. He spoke of trips to distant lands such as China, Persia, and India. Delighted by the stories, Rustichello started writing them down.

A portrait of Marco Polo in his forties

The rich man's name was Marco Polo. His book, *A Description of the World,* became very popular. For many Europeans the book was a window to the Far East and its traditions and geography. The Far East is made up of the countries of eastern Asia.

The explorer Christopher Columbus read Polo's book many times. He carried a copy when he went looking for a route to India in 1492.

Marco Polo was not the first European to travel to these lands. Other Europeans had been to them before. But Marco Polo did bring news about the customs of China and other Eastern lands to the people of Europe. He told about many things in the book, such as firecrackers, noodles, paper money, and coal. When Europeans began using these things, they forever changed the way people lived.

Early Life

Marco Polo was born around 1254. No one knows for sure the exact year or day. There are few written records from the 13th century. In fact, most of Marco's early life is a mystery because he didn't tell about himself in his book. But historians do know that his mother died when he was young. He was raised by an aunt and uncle.

Marco didn't meet his father until he was 15 years old. Niccolò Polo was a merchant. Merchants traveled all over the world to trade their goods. Before Marco was born, Niccolò went to Constantinople (now Istanbul) with his brother Maffeo to set up a business.

Because of wars and other dangers, the two brothers couldn't go back to Venice. Instead, they kept going east until they were in China. There they met the emperor, Kublai Khan. They became the Great Khan's ambassadors to Europe. Around 1269 the two men returned to Venice, where Niccolò finally met his son Marco.

8

Kublai Khan was a curious man. He had given Niccolò and Maffeo a letter for the Pope. In the letter, Kublai Khan asked for 100 people who could teach him about Christianity and other European learning. He also asked for some oil from a holy lamp in Jerusalem. But when the Polos got back to Venice, they learned that the Pope had died. They decided to wait for a new pope to be elected so they could return to Kublai Khan with the missionaries. Two years passed without a new pope. In 1271 the Polos decided they should just head back to China. They would tell Kublai Khan what had happened.

This time, Niccolò brought along his son Marco. The 17-year-old Marco wanted to travel with his father. Over the years he had been trained as a merchant, like the other men in his family. He had also learned how to read and write. He had studied math. He had also learned about foreign money and how to trade goods. These studies would help him trade in other countries. Marco wanted to join his father and travel around the world buying and selling things.

Kublai Khan asked the Polos to bring him holy oil from a lamp in Jerusalem.

Only a few days after they began their trip, the Polos were stopped by a messenger from Rome. The messenger brought news. A new pope, Gregory X (the Tenth), had been elected. The Polos turned back and gave the new pope the letter from the Great Khan. However, Gregory X couldn't find a hundred men to make the long trip to China.

Instead he sent Khan two friars. These were men who belonged to a church group. They did not go far. Shortly after the trip started, the friars became scared and turned back, leaving the Polos to go ahead on their own.

The two friars returned home.

 **11**

MARCO POLO'S ROUTE

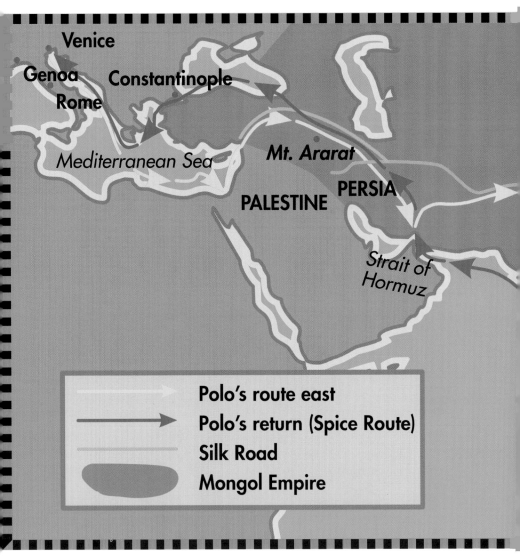

Venice

Genoa

Rome

Constantinople

Mediterranean Sea

Mt. Ararat

PALESTINE

PERSIA

Strait of Hormuz

→ Polo's route east
→ Polo's return (Spice Route)
— Silk Road
⬭ Mongol Empire

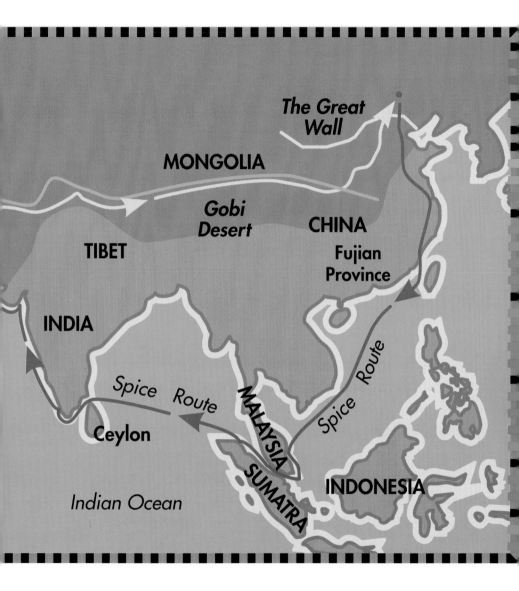

The Great
Wall

MONGOLIA

Gobi
Desert

CHINA

TIBET

Fujian
Province

INDIA

Spice Route

Ceylon

MALAYSIA

Spice Route

SUMATRA

INDONESIA

Indian Ocean

13

The Long Journey East

During the Middle Ages, about A.D. 500 to 1500, traveling to China from Europe took a very long time. A sea route was usually the best way to go. By land, travelers rode on horses and camels. Sometimes they had to cross mountains or deserts. Often thieves attacked and robbed them. So it is no wonder that the two friars sent by the Pope decided to turn back.

Marco Polo and his father and uncle were determined to reach China. First they took a ship across the Mediterranean Sea to Palestine (now Israel) in the Middle East. Then they rode camels into Persia (now Iran). They wanted to travel by sea from there to China, but the ships they would be sailing on were not safe.

On their way to China the Polos saw camels for the first time.

So the Polos decided to go by land across Asia. They rode camels across the deserts in Persia. They traveled through Afghanistan and other parts of Central Asia. They may have even stopped for a year in the mountains. Marco, or perhaps other members of his party, became sick and needed time to get well.

Soon the travelers reached the Silk Road, a famous travel route. Traders used this path to carry silks and spices between the Far East and Europe. The Polos rode all the way across China, as far as the Great Wall. The Great Wall had been built to keep out attackers. Finally they arrived in Shangdu, the summer home of Kublai Khan. The entire trip took three years.

On the trip Marco paid attention to everything around him. He met people of many different religions—Buddhists, Muslims, and Zoroastrians, among others. He learned new languages such as Turkish, Persian, Arabic, and Mongolian. The Mongolian language helped him when he met the Great Khan, because they could then talk easily to each other. Marco's language skills also helped him to talk to people in many parts of the Khan's empire.

The Great Wall of China

What happened on the Polos' journey east to Shangdu was told in *A Description of the World*. Marco Polo spent much time in the Pamir Mountains in Central Asia. This is an area too high even for birds. He discovered that fire didn't burn well, and water took longer to boil at such heights.

The Polos discovered that fire did not burn well at high altitudes.

When Marco Polo told about these things in his book, many readers thought these claims were not true. But we now know that all these things are true.

Marco also wrote about visiting Mt. Ararat in an ancient kingdom called Armenia. Many people believe this is the place where Noah's Ark finally landed after the flood. This story is told in the Bible.

In a region called Georgia (near Russia), Marco saw people using a strange oil as a fuel and medicine to soothe their skin. This oil was collected from the ground. In Marco's Europe oil usually came from olives or other plants. And it was used for eating. But the oil from the ground was not good as a food. This was the first time Europeans had heard of petroleum, the oil from which gasoline and motor oil are made. It still comes from the oil fields in Georgia.

The Polos also traveled across one of the largest deserts in the world, the Gobi in Asia. This was a very difficult part of the trip. The travelers had to spend long days crossing the dry desert to reach a place where they could find water. There were no places to stop for supplies. The travelers had to carry their food with them.

The Polos heard stories about spirits in the desert. They were thought to lead travelers off the path so that they would be lost forever.

It took the Polos a month to get through this dry land. Once they crossed the desert, they were in China. China was then under the control of Kublai Khan, a Mongol. Years before, Kublai Khan's grandfather, Genghis Khan, had invaded China and the areas around it. After Kublai Khan became emperor, he took over more lands to rule. So when Marco met Kublai Khan in 1275, he was meeting the king of the largest empire in the world.

A great temple in China

Kublai Khan, the Great Emperor

Kublai Khan's grandfather, Genghis Khan, invaded Northern China from Mongolia in 1211. Mongolia is a country in eastern Asia. It is north of China and south of Siberia. For the next two years, he kept moving. He went as far as today's Poland, Hungary, and Iran. He died in 1227, but not before founding the large empire that Kublai began to rule in 1260. This huge empire covered present-day southern China, Iran, and parts of India, Russia, and the Middle East. The Mongols also had some influence in the countries now known as Vietnam (Champa), Cambodia, and Myanmar (Burma).

Marco Polo arrives at Kublai Khan's palace.

Kublai Khan gives the Polos a golden tablet.

The Polos met Kublai Khan in Shangdu, China, at his summer court. In his book, Marco described how the Great Khan had built a large palace and city. He told of a marble building that had gold on the inside and a wall that surrounded 16 miles (25 km) of gardens. He also wrote about the animals, forests, and meadows inside the city walls.

⌇⌇⌇

When the Polos arrived at Kublai Khan's
court, they gave him letters from Pope Gregory X
(the Tenth). They also gave him holy oil from
Jerusalem. Then they introduced young Marco to
the emperor. Marco was only 21 years old, and the
Great Khan was about 60. Yet Kublai Khan liked
Marco right away. Marco impressed him with his
stories. He described the things he had seen on
the three- year-long trip.

The young Marco noticed that the Great Khan was bored by most of the visitors to his court. The ruler liked to hear about the sights, people, and cultures within his empire. Marco started to write about the many things he saw.

Soon the Khan was so impressed with what Marco wrote that he made Marco his emissary, or representative. Marco Polo was asked to travel to distant parts of the Mongol empire. Then he would report what he saw to the Great Khan.

Portrait of Marco Polo

Marco, the Careful Observer

Marco Polo and his father and uncle lived in China for the next 16 years. During that time they held positions in the Khan's court, which included many foreigners. They probably moved with the emperor to his winter palace in Khan-balik, today China's capital city of Beijing.

Some experts think Marco worked in the Khan's government. He might have had a job dealing with salt, a valuable material in the Middle Ages. Others think he was governor of Yangzhou, a large Chinese city. Still, it is hard to be sure about Marco's life since he rarely told about himself in *A Description of the World*. In any case, we do know that he traveled a great deal and saw parts of Asia that few Europeans had seen before.

The Great Wall of China is just one of the amazing sights Marco Polo described in his book.

On one trip, Marco went southward in China, to the region of Myanmar (Burma). On another journey, he saw eastern Persia (Iran). He tells about the mountain monasteries of Tibet in great detail, giving the world a clear picture of these hidden places. Monasteries are the homes of monks, people who devote their lives to religion. Marco's travels may have taken him as far as Japan, which he called Zipangu, and Vietnam, known then as Champa. It is likely that he didn't go to every place he described. He may have repeated stories told to him by other travelers. But what Marco Polo said in his book shows that he visited and saw most of the places he wrote about.

Marco Polo's accounts included far more than places and their landscapes. He also told about inventions in the Mongol empire. He was the first to write about the black stones mined from mountains. The stones were burned as fuel. We now know this was coal. When he wrote about the paper money in China, Europeans were still using heavy metal coins.

**Discoveries in the East:
coal, noodles, paper money,
gunpowder, and firecrackers**

The Chinese probably invented gunpowder in the 9th century. Gunpowder is used in making firecrackers. The powder is wrapped in paper tubes and then lighted.

The postal service Marco described was a group of horse riders and foot messengers who carried letters around the country.

Marco Polo wrote that the Chinese didn't eat bread but made noodles from wheat. When Europeans read about this, it started a new fashion in Marco's own country. Italians later learned how to make pasta by copying the Asians.

Heading Home

After many years in China, the Polos decided it was time to go home. Kublai Khan was old, and the Italians thought they might not be welcome in the Mongol empire after he died. They wanted to leave soon so that they could get outside the borders of the Khan's empire before it was too late.

About that time, a prince in Persia sent messengers to the Great Khan to ask for a new wife. His first wife had been a Mongol princess. Just before she died, her husband promised her that his next wife would be a member of her family. She was a descendant of Genghis Khan, just like Kublai. A descendant is someone born into a family. Because of this, it was Kublai's duty to choose and send the new wife. And someone had to take the princess to her new home in Persia.

The Polos may have seen a village like this one in Europe on their return trip.

The messengers sent by the Persian prince asked for the Polos, who were experienced travelers, to come with them. The Polos begged Kublai for the chance to go. Though he was not happy to see them leave, Kublai Khan finally gave his consent. He sent the Polos on the trip. But in order to leave, the Polos had to promise they would return.

In 1291 or 1292, the Polos sailed for India, the most direct way home. The Chinese boats they used were sturdy, so the trip across the ocean was much safer and faster than the long journey across land. Kublai sent them with 14 ships, some of which carried 250 men. They left from southern China, in what is now the Fujian province.

Along the way, the Polos stopped in Malaysia, Sumatra, Ceylon, and India. This route was known as the Spice Route. It was called this because boats carrying spices from Asia and India went along this route to Europe. The men saw many sights and met with many dangers, including pirates. By Marco's account, 600 men died along the way.

The Polos arrived in Hormuz, on the Persian Gulf, more than two years after leaving China. There they learned that the prince who had sent for

Marco Polo sailed on a Chinese boat, called a junk.

a new wife had died. The Mongol princess stayed in Persia and married the prince's son instead.

The Polos stayed in Persia for nine months. While they were there they learned that Kublai Khan had died in 1294. The Polos realized they would never go back to China. Instead, they left by boat for Venice and arrived home in 1295.

Marco in Venice

The Polos had been away from Venice for 24 years. But instead of a big celebration on their return, Marco and his father and uncle were greeted by people who didn't know who they were. Their clothes were dirty and torn. The relatives living in their house wouldn't let the strangers in. They thought the real Polos were dead.

Legend has it that Marco, Niccolò, and Maffeo then forced their way into the house and sliced open their clothes to show jewels they had hidden there. They convinced their relatives that they were truly the fine merchants who had left almost 25 years before. Now the relatives believed them. They gave a great feast to welcome the Polos home.

The busy port of Venice

Marco stayed in Venice, building his trading business and becoming richer. But only a year later, he had to fight to defend his trading rights. The city where he lived, Venice, went to war with Genoa, another Italian city. Each city wanted to control trading areas in the Mediterranean Sea.

Today both Venice and Genoa are part of Italy. Back in the 13th century, Italy was divided into many cities that had their own governments. These cities often went to war with each other over the right to trade goods in different parts of the world. Because Marco Polo was from Venice, he fought for that city.

Rich merchants like the Polos would pay to be in charge of galleys. These were ships that were used for war. The merchants would then be given a place on the ship while the war was fought. In this way, they advised the captain, since they were paying for the ship. In his forties, Marco went to war on a galley.

There was a battle between the Venetian fleet and the Genoese, and the Venetians lost. All their ships were captured. Seven thousand men were taken prisoner by the Genoese, including Marco Polo. He soon found himself in jail.

A Description of the World

Marco stayed in prison for a year, but he put his time to good use. He sent for the notebooks he had filled while in the service of Kublai Khan. Then, he began dictating stories about all the things he'd seen in his 24 years of travel to the writer Rustichello. The book was written in the language that most Italian writers used at the time. It was a mix of Italian and Old French.

Marco and Rustichello called the book *A Description of the World* because Marco wanted to do just that—describe the world he had seen. Over the years he had told many people of the wonderful sights in and around China, but no one believed him. In fact, they called him Marco Millions. They made fun of him because he always talked in big numbers and large distances when talking about his adventures. He wrote his book because he felt he had to prove that he was not lying.

In the 13th century, no one in Europe knew how to print books. Every copy of a book had to be written out by hand. People known as scribes did this work and sometimes added their own stories. Sometimes they changed Marco's words. Also, as the book was written in other languages, words were changed.

The original manuscript written during Marco's time in jail with Rustichello has been lost. Several copies of the book, probably from only a few years later, still exist. But historians can't be sure which book is most like the one Marco wrote. They can only piece together which stories Marco told and which were added by other scribes.

Regardless of which stories were accurate, the book became popular. It sold many copies and was read all around Europe. Marco described places and wonders that European people had never seen or heard about. He was also the first person to record Asia's geography. He named, in order, the countries he passed through on his way to and from China. His descriptions were so accurate, in fact, that the book became a guide for travelers for years to come.

A scribe copying Marco Polo's book

Since *A Description of the World* first came out in 1298, it has always been available for people to read. However, the title is often changed to *The Travels of Marco Polo* or *Il Milione (The Millions)*.

Just after he left prison, Marco Polo married a woman named Donata Badoer. Together they had three daughters, named Fantina, Bellala, and Moreta. Not much else is known about Marco except what experts can piece together from official documents. These include court papers and notes that belong to other people.

Marco Polo became very wealthy and very famous for his tales of his travels. Many people continued to think he made up his stories. It took centuries for historians to prove that most of what he said was entirely true.

Marco lived to be 70. Just before he died in Venice, on January 9, 1324, one of his daughters came to the dying man's bedside. She asked him to take back all of his false tales to save his family any more embarrassment. But Marco turned to her and said, simply, "I have not told half of what I saw."

Other Events of the 13th Century
(1201 – 1300)

1200   A famous Spanish poem, called *The Poem of the Cid*, is written.

1209   Cambridge University is started in England. This is a famous school.

1215   King John of England signs the Magna Carta. This agreement says that he will share his power with the people.

1228–1229   The Sixth Crusade is fought. The Crusades were wars fought between Christians and Muslims. The Christians wanted to take holy cities away from the Muslims.

1270   Paper is made in Italy. This is the first time paper is made in Europe.

1273   A great Italian thinker named Thomas Aquinas writes a book called *Summa Theologica*. It is used to teach Christianity.

1285   Eyeglasses are made in Italy for the first time.

1295   King Edward I of England starts the Model Parliament. This is a group of people who help the king make laws.

Time Line

1211   Genghis Khan invades China.

1215   Kublai Khan born.

1254   Niccolò and Maffeo Polo set out for Constantinople. They will later continue to China.

1254   Marco Polo born.

1260   Kublai Khan becomes Mongol emperor.

1269   Niccolò and Maffeo Polo return to Venice. Marco meets his father.

1271   Marco, Niccolò, and Maffeo Polo start out for China.

1275   The Polos arrive in Shangdu.

1291	The Polos leave China by boat and head for Persia.
1294	The Polos reach Persia.
1294	Kublai Khan dies.
1295	The Polos return to Venice.
1296	Marco goes to war and is captured by the Genoese. He begins dictating *A Description of the World* to Rustichello.
1298	*A Description of the World* is published.
1324	Marco Polo dies.

Glossary

ambassador (am-BASS-uh-dor) An official person chosen to represent one country or government on behalf of another country or government

court The councillors and officers who advise a king, queen, emperor, or empress

culture (KUHL-chur) The customs, beliefs, and traditions of a group of people based on their race, religion, or society

descendant (dee-SEN-dant) Someone born directly into a family, such as a child or grandchild

emissary (EM-uh-say-ree) An official government representative

galley A long, low ship, powered only by oars, used for war and trading in the Mediterranean Sea

Genoese (JEN-oh-ees) A citizen of Genoa

Great Wall (of China) A giant stone barrier, 1,400 miles (2,250 km) long and 30 feet (9.1 m) high, begun in 215 B.C. in Northern China to keep out attackers

manuscript (MAN-you-skript) A book that has been written out by hand or typed instead of printed

merchant A buyer or seller of products for profit; a trader

Middle Ages The period of European history from A.D. 500 to 1500

missionary (MI-shun-ay-ree) A person sent to live among the people of another country to teach them about a religion

monastery (MON-uh-stay-ree) A house for monks, men whose lives are devoted to religion

ritual (RIH-chew-uhl) A ceremony, act, or custom repeated for religious or cultural reasons

Rustichello (roos-tee-KELL-ow) A famous writer from Pisa whom Marco Polo became friendly with in prison

scribe A person who copies out manuscripts by hand; in the Middle Ages, often a monk

Silk Road The series of roads, caravan tracks, and mountain passes that connected Europe with eastern Asia, along which were carried goods, such as silk and spices, for trading

Spice Route The sea route, following the southern coasts of Asia, India, and Mediterranean Europe, along which traders traveled between Europe and the Far East

Index